TORTEVAL SCHOOL IN EXILE

1. Frank Harry Le Poidevin (1901-1975)
Headmaster, Torteval School, 1940-1946
In exile 21st June 1940 - 24th July 1945

Torteval School in Exile

*The story of a Guernsey School
evacuated shortly before the
German Occupation of 1940-45
and its establishment at
Alderley Edge near Manchester*

Nick Le Poidevin

ELSP

Published in 2010 by
ELSP
16A New St John's Road
St Helier
Jersey   JE2 3LD

Origination by Seaflower Books, Jersey

Printed by Cromwell Press Group
Trowbridge, Wiltshire

ISBN 978-1-906641-22-1

All enquiries and correspondence
relating to this book should be
directed to the author at

Le Morpaye
Les Martins
St Pierre du Bois
Guernsey   GY7 9AN

CONTENTS

REFERENCES

Because this work is based almost entirely upon the Log Book of Torteval School in Exile (and enclosures found with it) and upon the writer's personal recollections, very little reference is made of other material and where it is this is noted in the text. There are two exceptions, books to which reference is made on more than one occasion:

1. Cruickshank, C.: *The German Occupation of the Channel Islands*. (Published for the Trustees of the Imperial War Museum by The Guernsey Press Co. Ltd., 1975).

2. Von Aufsess, Baron: *The von Aufsess Occupation Diary*, edited and translated by Kathleen J. Nowlan (Published by Phillimore & Co. Ltd., 1985).

LIST OF ILLUSTRATIONS, DOCUMENTS, etc.

AUTHOR'S FOREWORD

In 1940, each parish in Guernsey had its parish school or schools. On 21st June that year, Guernsey's smallest parish, Torteval, had a school with 101 pupils on its roll. Two days earlier, in expectation of an imminent German invasion, the States of Guernsey arranged for the voluntary evacuation of all children of school age. So it was that, in the very early hours of Friday 21st June, 35 of those children left their homes and travelled with their headmaster, Frank Le Poidevin, from their school building to an unknown future in England. This Torteval School in Exile did not return until late July 1945.

The German army occupied Guernsey on Sunday 30th June 1940. On 22nd July, Torteval School in Occupation opened under its previous headmaster, Captain Ernest Boon. So it was that during the period 1940-1945, the parish of Torteval had two schools and two headmasters, each unsure of the other's existence, some three hundred miles apart, and out of communication with each other. What I have written concerns Torteval School in Exile. It is based upon the Log Book kept by its headmaster during that period and upon my recollections as his son and a pupil at his school. I leave it to another to tell the story of Torteval School in Occupation.

I dedicate this narrative to the people of Torteval who lived through that period, and to the memories of its parish Rector, Reverend Edmondson Nelson Greenhow, and of the two Headmasters of its school, Captain Ernest Boon, of the School in Occupation, and Frank Le Poidevin, of the School in Exile.

Note

There are a number of plates accompanying this narrative. The Log Book is hand written and now seventy years old and is fragile. Some of the enclosures are in an even worse state! For that reason, I have not made photographic copies of these, but provided transcripts. I hope that readers will understand. Some transcripts of letters are of those appearing as enclosures, others are from the Log Book itself where my father had written the text of a letter received or sent.

Guernsey
May 2010

ABOUT GUERNSEY AND GUERNSEY WORDS

In 1204, the Channel Islands chose allegiance to the English Crown. They govern themselves in domestic matters but the United Kingdom is responsible for their foreign affairs. The Islands are not part of the United Kingdom nor are in the European Union. Guernsey and Jersey have separate governments and laws. **Alderney** and Sark come under Guernsey but generally control their domestic affairs.

Guernsey's government is the **States of Deliberation** (the **States**). Its members are called **Deputies**. Its law court is the **Royal Court**. The **Bailiff** is civil head of Guernsey and senior judge of the Royal Court where he is assisted by **Jurats** who form a permanent jury.

Guernsey has 10 civil **parishes**: St Peter Port, St Sampson's, the Vale, the Castel, St Saviour's, St Peter's (in the Wood), Torteval, the Forest, St Martin's, and St. Andrew's. Every parish has a council of 12, the **Douzaine,** assisted by two **Constables**. The minister of each parish Church, (Anglican since 1662), is its **Rector**.

Guernsey's one town, St. Peter Port, is usually called 'Town'. Its two schools are **Amherst** and **Vauvert**. Its harbour has a quay called the **White Rock** and passengers use the **New Jetty**. The northern seaward approach is through a narrow passage, the **Little Russel**.

The native language of Guernsey, **Patois**, is a form of Norman French; it is not degenerate French but a distinct language. Few persons now use it. At one time modern French was the official language of Guernsey but now English is the language of its inhabitants.

INTRODUCTION

My late father, Frank Harry Le Poidevin, was headmaster of Torteval School from 1940 until 1946. Amongst his papers, I found the Log Book of the school that covers the events from the time of the evacuation in June 1940 until it merged with Alderley Edge Primary School, Cheshire, in April 1942. It is a public document, but before placing it in the safe hands of the Island Archivist I have chosen to publish edited extracts from it along with my commentary. Indeed, without such a commentary, the Log Book would have far less meaning to a casual reader. I am not preparing a transcript of it for this and for another reason. The Log Book contains personal references to children still alive or whose close family and friends remain alive. In my view such matters should not be made public.

What I write in my commentary is based upon my recollection of events of seventy years ago as seen through my eyes as the child of its headmaster and in it I try to emphasise the problems as faced by him and my mother as they led a party of schoolchildren to an uncertain future on that fateful morning of 21st June. What I write draws almost entirely upon the Log Book, its enclosures, and my own memory including what my parents told me. I acknowledge assistance from Mrs Faith Feak, daughter of the late Reverend Greenhow who was the Rector of Torteval before, during, and after the German Occupation and from Mr Peter Boon, grandson of Captain Ernest Boon, headmaster of Torteval School from 1930-1939 and again from July 1940 of Torteval School in Occupation.

At the outset, I emphasise that the school Log Book is not a diary. Nowhere does it express my father's thoughts nor does he offer any commentary on the events as they unfolded. It is those thoughts that I seek to convey. I do not set out to give yet another history of the evacuation, occupation, and liberation. For this I refer readers to the official account by Dr Charles Cruickshank[1] compiled after access to both British and German sources.

One valuable source of information about my father's thoughts are the enclosures that are contained in the Log Book, they are not part of it but so often when seeking to edit an older book or diary one can glean a lot from the odd bits of paper enclosed in it.

I express many of my own impressions and opinions. Historians may say that these were erroneous, but I hope that others that read it will understand how the events of some seventy years ago have dominated the thinking of a person into their later years. It is perhaps of passing interest to read of another's deprivations, whatever they were, during those war years. It is, I suggest, of greater interest and value to consider how the life of a person can be shaped by the circumstances of their earlier and formative years. It is the latter that I seek to convey.

Since many younger readers will read this, I shall make some preliminary comments about life in Guernsey in early 1940. I hope that this will assist them in appreciating the way in which we lived in those days and assist their understanding of the events that I describe. Torteval, like most country parishes, was very much a self-contained unit. It had its Parish School, its Church, its Chapel, and most people lived and worked in the same parish as where they were born and raised. At that time, and indeed for some years after the war, Torteval was far from being a dormitory for persons working in Town, nor was it a place to which people retired from elsewhere. It was a community of people who lived off its land or from the sea. One of the focal points of the community was the parish Rector. At that time the Rectors of the ten parishes were members of the States of Deliberation. My recollection of Reverend Greenhow is that he visited every home in the parish irrespective of whether they worshipped at the Church, the Chapel, or anywhere at all. As will be mentioned later, it was with him that my father attempted to communicate the affairs of the evacuees.

Lifestyles, whether in Guernsey, or for that matter on the other side of the Channel, were much simpler than those of today. Foodstuffs that we now take for granted were unknown even to a wealthy elite. Exotic food was not flown in from all over the globe. We knew oranges, lemons, and bananas because they came by sea. We did not know mangoes, papaws, avocado pears or sweet potatoes. Few people had seen an aubergine, a sweet pepper, a bulb of fennel, or a root of celeriac. For fish we ate conger, mackerel, or herring, not salmon or monkfish. For meat we ate mostly Guernsey beef with its deep yellow fat, not pallid imported meat. There were not any deep freezers and few homes had refrigerators. We ate what was in season. Many homes had land devoted to vegetables and fruit and maybe they kept chickens or fattened a pig. We did not have supermarkets, pre-packed food, or pre-cooked meals. We did not go out to restaurants unless away from home, and pub lunches were unknown. People of those days would shake their heads in utter disbelief to hear of how we now have daily imports not only of frozen food, but also of ready-made meals and even of fresh sandwiches, all in extravagant throwaway packaging. Many houses relied on weekly visits by the butcher, fishmonger, and greengrocer and more frequent visits by the milkman and the baker. Some homes had electricity and maybe cooked by it, others relied upon mains gas or paraffin for both cooking and lighting. No such thing as a microwave oven! Coal fires were the commonest way for heating houses.

Communications, too, were very different. Most homes had a wireless, either running off the mains or powered by lead accumulators. There was neither commercial nor local radio and we relied on BBC London. Radio was not used, as it is now, as a means of communication. Television was not known in Guernsey and was in its early days in the UK. Telephones were available, but not all homes had landlines, – no mobiles or text messages! We did not have direct dialling. To telephone Town from Torteval one contacted the operator at St Peter's exchange who would put one through to the Town exchange as soon as a line was free. Calls to the UK could take some time to connect. On the other hand, postal services were quick and efficient. Letters were a general means of communication but where speed was essential telegrams were used. In those days such things as the Internet as a means of communication and source of information were not even in a person's wildest dreams.

Although some people in Guernsey possessed a car, for the majority the means of travel was by bus or for the more active a bicycle or possibly a motorbike. As I have mentioned, it was more usual for tradesmen to deliver food than for us to go to a shop for our every need. Children walked to school or, if a child in Torteval were schooled in Town, then they would use the bus or a pushbike. The modern system of carrying children to school in a dedicated school bus or in a gas-guzzling 4x4 was not in our contemplation.

Another point that I must mention is the matter of photography. By 1940, many families possessed a camera. It was usually a simple affair such as a Kodak 'Brownie' that took black and white photographs. These were taken to a chemist for developing and prints were made from the original negative. In consequence, many families still possess photographs of pre-war days, generally of children growing up or of family outings. My parents did not take a camera with them at the time of the evacuation, making a photographic record was the least of their worries, and in any event film was extremely difficult to obtain in the war years. Consequently I am unable to include with this narrative any photographs taken during the five years away. Possibly a number of school photographs were taken by professional photographers, but I cannot trace any. Modern readers must realise that colour photography was not generally available until after the war years and such things as video cameras and digital photography arrived much later.

Knowledge of life outside Guernsey, or even outside the Parish, was something not well known to many of the children that were evacuated. We knew of the outside world from pictures in books and from visits to the cinema when there was always a news programme before the main feature. We also knew of the outside world from photographs taken by those who had travelled, generally in the course of work or in the armed forces. For many families in the pre-war years it was unheard of to go away for a holiday. Air travel was in its infancy and the package holiday was yet to arrive. If one had to travel one did so by mail boat and onward by steam train. Drive-on car ferries were unknown. However, a good point was a freedom of travel; one went to the New Jetty, bought a ticket to travel to any rail station in the UK at a pre-set price, and simply got on the boat without any identity or security check. In this modern age Guernsey in becoming a fortress island in matters of travel and buying a ticket is an art in itself.

Prior to the evacuation, my parents had no personal knowledge of life in England apart from time spent at teachers' training college, on honeymoon in the Mendips, and a visit to see the sights of London. One consequence was that they had no experience of the English class system. In Guernsey we were taught to treat certain people with respect but in another sense we saw each other as equals in our possession of human dignity. In the evacuation years, exposure to the English class system was to have a profound effect on my parents, upon my mother in particular. In Guernsey then, as indeed now, one rose to a senior position in public life by reason of ability rather than by accident of birth. We found at Alderley Edge a rigid class system and my parents were totally unprepared, as was I as a child, for exposure to it.

One final and general point. In the days leading up to the German Occupation, the Royal Court had assumed executive powers. As Cruickshank[1] explains, three civil servants were dispatched to the United Kingdom to look after the needs of evacuees. My father had dealings with two of these, Mr J. P. Robert and Mr R. G. Harwood, as will appear later in my narrative. Both returned to Guernsey after the war. Mr Harwood, uncle of Advocate Peter Harwood of the 'Harwood Report', was invited by Sir John Leale to join his Firm. Mr Robert remained with the civil service and played a large part in setting up Guernsey's Social Security Authority. In his retirement, he developed a wonderful garden at Le Chêne.

Part One

EVACUATION

I was five years old at the outset of War. My first memory of it was of my father explaining to me on an atlas the German invasion of Poland and showing me how to put on a gasmask and the need to take it with me whenever I left home. At that time we were living in St Martin's at the junction of Les Frieteaux and Rue Poudreuse. I think it was my father who planted the pine tree that now stands as a mature specimen on that corner. Being below the age for compulsory education, I attended a kindergarten in Mount Row run by a Miss Baker.

My father was an assistant master at Amherst until January 1940 when be became headmaster at Torteval subsequent to the retirement of Captain Boon. At that time, cars were for the wealthy and my father travelled to and from Torteval each day on his bicycle. On what was, it would seem, the afternoon of 19th June he took me with him to Torteval on the back of his bicycle and I was enrolled at that school. I remember going there with him, although I was too young to understand why. I also remember sitting in a classroom of mostly older children, none of whom I knew. Amazingly, on the eve of the evacuation there were 101 pupils on the school roll. This is striking because compulsory education started at six and finished at the age of 14. It shows how many children there were in the parish at that time. The school itself occupied the building next to the Church, now used as the Douzaine Room, although the infants were accommodated in the buildings attached to the Methodist Chapel across the valley.

I learned subsequently from my father that he and other head teachers had been called in to the Education Office and having been sworn to secrecy were told that a decision had been made to evacuate as many children as possible as quickly as arrangement could be made, although the final decision would remain with individual parents. The reason for that meeting in Torteval on June 19th was to acquaint parents of the evacuation plans and to find out how many children were to be evacuated. Enclosed in the Log Book was a copy of the evacuation notice issued by the Bailiff, Victor Carey, on that day. It is somewhat in tatters these 70 years on, so I present a transcript in Plate 3. It reminds us of how hurriedly the decision was made to evacuate and of how little each child could take, essentially a change of clothes, some nightwear, some food and a gas mask, effectively what the child could carry. Readers will notice that there was not any mention of toys or of family photographs. Another enclosure in the Log Book is some labels presumably designed to tie to children and their belongings (Plate 2).

72 children were scheduled to travel but only 35 left as planned. Mrs Faith Feak, daughter of the late Reverend Edmondson Greenhow, then Rector of Torteval, kindly gave me a copy of a letter from my father to Peter, her brother, written in September 1940. With her permission, I am depositing it with the States' Archivist along with the Log Book. In that letter my father made the caustic remark that clocks in Torteval must have stopped because less than half of those scheduled to travel did in fact do so. This is an appropriate point to mention that Peter Greenhow, then a sergeant in the RAF, was lost in action somewhere in North Africa. His name is inscribed on the parish war memorial.

That night of 20/21st June 1940 must have been an agonising time for parents and I am sure that many had second thoughts and wondered whether to put their children on the bus leaving the school for the harbour in the very early hours of that Friday morning. All these years on, it is sobering to speculate on the thoughts of those parents that did not put their children on the bus at that early hour of 21st June. Had they made the right choice? We know that some left independently during the course of the following days, but what of the others who learned of the air raid at the White Rock the following Friday evening and found themselves occupied two days later? It was perhaps only then that the reality of their decisions became apparent. The School buildings were considered too small to be worth requisitioning by the occupying forces and, as mentioned later, the school reopened on 22nd July and continued in Guernsey under its previous headmaster, Captain Boon.

Many parents and indeed people as a whole in Guernsey were uncertain as to whether to evacuate or not. Cherbourg had fallen and the Germans occupied the Cotentin Peninsular but many in Guernsey believed that this was a temporary set back and that the evacuation was a precautionary measure and no more. My mother made a last minute decision to leave and even then believed that she was simply helping with the party of evacuees and would return shortly to Guernsey. For that reason she never said goodbye to her parents although they lived close by. My father's parents lived in St Sampson's and I think that he cycled down to see them. That would have been the last time that he saw his father.

My father probably went back to Torteval in the evening of the 20th. I remember my mother waking me in the middle of the night and a bus from Torteval stopping outside our house. It stopped again to allow my mother to put our house key through her parents' letterbox. When we reached the harbour, it was low water on a spring tide and we had to go down slippery steps in the dark to a lower landing of the New Jetty in order to embark on the *Sheringham*, a cattle boat. Along with the 35 children from Torteval and their 7 teachers and helpers were 393 children and 49 adults from the Vale Junior School; 75 children and 12 adults from the Vale Infants; 48 children and 4 adults from Alderney States School; 17 children and 7 adults from St. Anne's Convent School, Alderney, and a mother and child, making a total of 569 children and 80 adults.

We left at 3.15 a.m. on Friday 21st June. The boat was not a passenger boat, it was seriously overcrowded, and the crossing was rough. Many of us were badly seasick. At one point we were under cover for two hours because enemy aircraft were reported off the Isle of Wight. We eventually reached Weymouth, I think in the early afternoon, and we saw what for most of us was our first sight of a train standing on Weymouth Quay. It was not ours for we were taken to a reception centre somewhere along the sea front and after medical examinations had some very welcome food. Most of us had long since eaten the food that we brought from Guernsey and a lot of that ended with the fishes!

We were then taken to Weymouth Town railway station and it was only when the train was under way that the guard told my parents of our destination. The name meant little to them. I remember feeling very alone and unhappy. My parents had to maintain discipline and they could not show me any especial favours or treat me any differently from the other children who were now separated from their parents. I could not 'pull rank' and claim to be the headmaster's son. This was to be the inevitable pattern of things.

The train puffed its way north and we saw for the first time the vastness of England's rolling countryside dotted with strange coloured cattle. We slumbered as the train rolled on through the short summer night and we reached our destination of Rochdale at 5.40 a.m. the next morning, Saturday 22nd June.

From discussions with Mr R. J. Raymond of Alderney, who has been researching the evacuation from the Alderney standpoint, I have established that it is highly probable that the Alderney children were with us on the same train. Upon arrival at Rochdale it appears that we were taken to different reception centres, although after two weeks both States schools were moved to Alderley Edge in Cheshire. Those of us from Torteval were taken to Horse Carrs. With help of the Internet I have found that this was a 19th century mill owner's mansion and it remains standing having since been used for various social purposes including an evangelical school. It seemed very large to us. It was set in grounds with extensive shrubberies of laurels and rhododendrons. These separated it from a mill that belched smoke from its tall round brick chimney. Indeed my memories of Rochdale are of pale blue skies, quite unlike the deep midsummer blue of Guernsey, of tall chimneys sending out smoke, and, as a consequence, of getting our clothes and our hands filthy dirty through playing on the grass or in the shrubberies. My one recollection of visiting Rochdale town to search out clothing is likewise of a pale blue sky and smoky haze. One shop that we visited was Littlewoods, at that time a chain of clothing stores. It has since moved on to the more profitable businesses of football pools and mail order catalogues! My father also managed to buy some infant reading books at Woolworths.

It is possible that the children from the Vale Schools travelled with us on the same special train from Weymouth and that it was divided at Crewe. I cannot be sure but I say this because the Vale children went to Wigan where they stayed until 7th July when they were moved mostly to Nantwich, Cheshire. (See Wigan Heritage Service Publication No. 42, April-July 2006, page 13 etc., @ www.wlct.org/Culture/ Heritage/pf42).

My father's Log Book contains the names and details of those who evacuated and I give these in Plate 4. Included in these details are those contained later in the Log Book of children who left the school during those five years. To put the evacuation in perspective it is instructive to note the ages of the evacuees and to imagine the whole episode as in unfolded in late June 1940. The youngest, Madelaine Brehaut, was some three months short of her sixth birthday. The oldest, Nicholas Robilliard, was two months after his thirteenth. I invite readers to look at children in this age group whom they know and to imagine the scene at Torteval School in those early hours of 21st June 1940 as the children boarded a bus and their parents bade them farewell. Imagine also the feelings of the group of accompanying adults as they learned a few days later that the German occupation had begun. This was no trip to a Scout or Girl Guide camp with the promise of a return. It was a venture into the unknown both for the children, their carers, and for those who bade them goodbye.

We shared Horse Carrs with part of the States Intermediate School for Girls. The Log Book notes that the building was quite crowded but it mentions and names the Lancashire people who helped us to settle in and commends both them and the various helpers from Guernsey who made every effort to look after the children and keep them clean.

My parents spoke very little to me about the evacuation, or indeed about the whole five years away, I know it affected them both, particularly my mother. I often wonder how they must have felt finding themselves in a strange place with the responsibility of children separated from their parents. I know that my mother managed to phone hers during the first week away but soon all that contact came to an abrupt end. The Log Book notes that on Sunday, 30th June, all children attended Church or Chapel and my father notes that evening prayers were encouraged. What it does not note is that on that same Sunday the German occupation began and with it all hope of communication with parents and loved ones in Guernsey. Maybe my father did not mention it because he considered it irrelevant to the business of running the school.

I have no particular recollection of being told about the occupation of Guernsey, but I wonder how my father broke the news to the children and what their thoughts would have been? I don't think that we knew at the time of the German air attack on tomato lorries lined up at the White Rock on the evening of Friday 28th June. I mention this attack with its tragic loss of 33 lives for two reasons. Firstly, those in Guernsey did not appreciate the imminence of the German invasion. It was business as usual. At the time of the attack, the mail boat, *Isle of Sark*, was in the harbour on a regular sailing to England and tomatoes were awaiting shipment. Secondly, it draws attention to a matter that only becomes clear in Cruickshank's history[1], namely that although a decision had been made to demilitarise the Channel Islands, because of some administrative blunders this decision was not conveyed to the German government in time to prevent this unnecessary loss of life. This again illustrates the general uncertainty amongst those remaining in Guernsey as to what was happening. I am sure that many wrong decisions were made on the spur of the moment by ordinary people due to the lack of information. That air raid closed the door to further departures from the Island. The mail boat did not return and German forces arrived.

This is an appropriate point to record that shortly after

the evacuation, Torteval School re-opened in Guernsey with its former headmaster, Captain Ernest Boon, being recalled. As far as one can gather it had about 50 pupils. Along with many others, Captain Boon, now elderly and in failing health, was deported to Germany and sadly died at Biberach in October 1943, shortly after his arrival there. I have no knowledge of how the school continued but my late wife, who started school there during the Occupation, remembered being taught German.

I suspect that my father's attitude was also one of 'business as usual' and a feeling that schooling must go on to keep minds occupied. On Monday 1st July at the invitation of Mr. Royds, Director of Education at Rochdale my father visited Cronkeyshaw School where two rooms were placed at his disposal. (See Plate 5). We started there next day and continued until Friday, apart from a few children that had contracted German measles. It was a strange experience as a minority group in a larger school resounding in Lancashire accents and with unfamiliar behaviour.

During the course of that week a number of the original party left us. Apart from children, as noted in the List of Evacuees (Plate 4), some helpers also left us. There was then notification, not recorded in the Log Book, that we were to be transferred to Alderley Edge. However, it does note that on the evening of Saturday 6th July, the boys had their hair cut and received a good leg and body wash prior to transfer.

We were taken to Rochdale station on the morning of Sunday 7th July and entrained for Alderley Edge where we arrived later that morning, I presume that the party from Alderney States school, but not the convent, were with us on the same train although this is not mentioned by my father since the two schools were completely separate at that time. My father told me that upon arrival he was greeted with a nervous gentleman stammering out 'Parlez-vous anglais?'

He was taken aback, or maybe relieved by my father's reply 'Damn side better than you do!' This anecdote related to me by my father not only shows the general ignorance of the Channel Islands on the part of the villagers but much more commendably the hospitality and willingness of its good people to accommodate a group of unknown children who might not be speakers of English.

Upon arrival we assembled in the car park area outside the up platform and allocated to billets. My father did his best to keep family ties unbroken and I know that during our stay at Alderley Edge he and my mother did everything possible to ensure that the Torteval children were well cared for by their foster parents for what appeared then to be a very uncertain future. This care included entertaining the Torteval children in rotation to tea at our billet and, when Red Cross messages started, helping them to communicate with their families in Guernsey.

2. *Label found enclosed with the Log Book and presumably used to label children and their belongings*

Overleaf: 3. Transcript of an original copy of the typewritten Evacuation Notice found enclosed with the School Log Book, (annotations in italics).

EVACUATION FROM GUERNSEY
NOTICE

Arrangements are being made for the evacuation of (1) children of school age and (2) children under school age to reception areas in the United Kingdom under Government arrangements.

The evacuation is expected to take place to-morrow the 20th. June, 1940.

The mothers of children under school age will be allowed to accompany their children.

Parents of schoolchildren are to attend the school attended by their children at 7.00 p.m. to-day to notify their willingness or otherwise for the evacuation of their children.

Parents of children under school age who desire their children evacuated must give their name and address of such children to the Rector or Vicar of their Parish by 8 p.m. to-day. The Rector will prepare lists accordingly and will transmit them by 10 p.m. to the Bailiff's Office.

Other persons (other than men of military age) desirous of being evacuated must register their names and addresses with the Constables of their parish at the Parish Douzaine Room as soon as possible and at latest by 8 p.m. to-day.

All men of military age i.e. from 18 to 41 years *(Manuscript amendment to 20 to 33 years)*, who desire to be evacuated must register their names and addresses with the Constables of their Parish at the Parish Douzaine Room by 9 p.m. THEY ARE VERY STRONGLY URGED TO DO SO.

Children should take with them on evacuation the following articles:-
Gas masks
2 ration books (current and new one)

Besides the clothes which the child will be wearing, which should include and overcoat or mackintosh, a complete change of clothing should be carried. The following is suggested :-

Girls	Boys
One vest or combinations.	One vest.
One pair of knickers.	One shirt with collar.
One bodice.	One pair of pants.

One petticoat.
Two pairs of stockings.
Handkerchiefs.
Slip or blouse.
Cardigan.

One pullover or Jersey.
One pair of knickers.
Handkerchiefs.
Two pairs of socks or stockings.

Additional for all
Night attire; comb; towel; soap; face-cloth; tooth-brush; and, if possible, boots and shoes and plimsolls.

Blankets must not be taken.

Rations for the journey: Sandwiches (egg or cheese); Packets of nuts and seedless raisins; Dry biscuits (with little packets of cheese); Barley sugar (rather than chocolate); Apple; Orange.

Parents of children to be evacuated must attend at the school attended by their children at 9.00 a.m. to-morrow the 20th June to receive instructions as to the final arrangements to be complied with.

Parents of children under school age will attend at the Parish School of the Parish in which they reside at 10 a.m. to-morrow the 20th June to receive similar instructions.

It will not be possible, on account of the danger of air raids, to permit masses of people to congregate at the harbour and accordingly parents must say au-revoir to their children at their homes or at the Schools. The public will not be permitted to approach the harbour.

Transport to the Harbour will be provided as necessary.

On registration for the evacuation of children or adults, it must be stated whether or not financial provision can be made for the maintenance of the evacuee in the United Kingdom and whether or not the evacuee can go to a relative or friend there and the name and address of that relative or friend must be given.

(Annotation in Headmaster's writing - 6/- or less/or more)

VICTOR G. CAREY.
Bailiff of Guernsey.

June 19th. 1940.

4. Names of Torteval School children and helpers evacuated on 21st June 1940

This list has been compiled from the Log Book. Dates of birth are omitted. Addresses are given either as the address in Torteval or of the Parish where the child or adult resided. The groups are as given in the Log Book. It is possible that each group was assigned to one or more helpers.

Name	Age at time of Evacu-ation	Address	Remarks
Group I			
Carré, Neville	7	Glenview	
Edwards, Kenneth	6	Les Simons	Left 15.10.40 - claimed by parents, St. Helen's.
Gallienne, David	6	Meadow View	
Mahy, Roy	6	Le Colombier	Claimed by parents 05.7.40
Paint, André	7	(St. Peter's)	
Roussel, Bernard	7	(St. Peter's)	
Ashplant, Joan	6	Rosedale	Claimed by parents 05.7.40
Brehaut, Madelaine	5	Melrose	
Queripel, Joyce	6	Paradise	
Group II			
Brehaut, Grace	8	Melrose	Left 27.8.43 - scholarship to Girls' Intermediate, Rochdale.
Brehaut, Molly Jean	8	La Neuve Maison	
Duquemin, Hazel	7	La Vallée	
Edwards, Ethel	7	Les Simons	
Robilliard, Loïs	7	Les Douvres	Left 30.10.42 - scholarship to Girls' Intermediate, Rochdale.
Edwards, Sylvester	8	Les Simons	Left 29.10.40 - claimed by parents at St.Helen's.
Le Poidevin, Nicholas	6	(St Martin's)	Scholarship to Elizabeth College. Left 01.9.44
Robilliard, Walter	8	Les Jehans	
Torode, Oswald	9	Les Jehans	
Tostevin, Gordon	? b.1931	Glenview	Claimed by parents 05.7.40
Stephens, Donald	7	Trinity Cottages	Claimed by parents 05.7.40
Moore, Raymond	8	(St. Peter's)	

Group III

Name	Age	Location	Notes
Gallienne, Brenda	10	Rougeval	Claimed by parents 05.7.40
Le Lacheur, Sheila	9	La Rocque	Claimed by parents 05.7.40
Brehaut, Norman	10	Melrose	Left 19.09.41 - scholarship to Boys' Intermediate, Oldham.
Edwards, Stanley	11	Les Simons	Left 29.10.40 - claimed by parents at St. Helen's.
Gallienne, George	9	St. Cloud	Left 09.02.42 - scholarship to Boys' Intermediate, Oldham.
Gallienne, Donald	10	Meadow View	Also left 09.02.42 - scholarship as above.
Le Prevost, Kenneth	10	(St. Peter's)	Left 17.2.44 - gardening.
Stephens, Richard	10	Trinity Cottages	Claimed by parents, 05.07.40. Subsequently awarded 4-year scholarship to IOW secondary school.

Group IV

Name	Age	Location	Notes
Edwards, Sheila	12	Les Simons	Left 29.10.40 - claimed by parents at St. Helen's.
Brehaut, Walter	12	Les Fontaines	Left 23.11.42 - farming.
Brouard, John	12	Rougeval	Claimed by father 06.7.40.
Robilliard, Nicholas	13	Les Jehans	Left 10.4.41 - farming.

Other

Name	Age	Location	Notes
Courts, Audrey	12	(St Martin's)	Daughter of Mrs. Courts, teacher from Girls' Intermediate.
Moore, Olive	10	Trinity Cottages	

Teachers and helpers

Name	Age	Location	Notes
Le Poidevin, Frank	38	(St Martin's)	Headmaster
Le Poidevin, Gladys (Jean)	39	(St Martin's)	Helper, wife of headmaster
Corbet, Miss Grace	51	(St. Peter's)	First assistant. Left 31. 10. 42.
Courts, Mrs. L.	47	(St Martin's)	Infant mistress and supply teacher. Left 04.7.40.
Renault, Miss Wilma	16	(Forest)	Monitress. Left 06.7.40.
Greenhow, Miss Mary	19	Torteval Rectory	Helper. Left 05.7.40 to join aunt at Stoke-on-Trent.
Courts, Mr. W.	50	(St Martin's)	Helper, husband of Mrs. Courts.

COUNTY BOROUGH OF ROCHDALE
EDUCATION COMMITTEE

Education Office,
Townhead
Rochdale

28th June, 1940.

Dear Sir,

I have arranged for your children to be accommodated at Cronkeyshaw Junior School.

I shall be glad if you will call at the school on Monday afternoon next, 1st July, in order to discuss the final arrangements with the head teacher (Miss Thompson) with a view to the children commencing attendance on Tuesday next.

Yours faithfully,
(signed - A. Royds)

Directorof Education

Mr. F. H. LePoidevin,
C/o Horse Carrs,
Falings Road,
ROCHDALE.

5. Transcript of a letter from Rochdale Education Office concerning accommodation of children at Cronkeyshaw School.

Part Two

ESTABLISHMENT

I must now say something about Alderley Edge that was to be our home for the next five years of our lives. It is a modern village, a product of the railway built in the nineteenth century. It is situated in Cheshire some 10 miles south of Manchester between the much older villages of Wilmslow and Nether Alderley. One reason for its building was to assist financing of the railway from London into Manchester. It did this by providing homes for the emerging wealthy industrialist class at a pleasant site away from the grime of Lancastrian industry and yet within a short rail journey of its centre. Along with the great villas that were built on higher ground and lesser ones built on its slopes, there was a range of buildings to accommodate those who serviced the needs of the new moneyed elite. The main road south from Manchester ran through the new village and became and remains a wide shop-lined road on a sweeping curve with broad footpaths. To its east are Victorian detached and semi-detached houses for the lower middle class artisans, shopkeepers and professionals. To its west and between it and the railway line are narrow streets of terraced brick houses. These accommodated the hundreds needed to service the wealthy, either as domestic servants, or gardeners, or to work generally on the infrastructure of the new village. Even these had social distinctions, the better ones being to the south whilst the lesser ones were nearer to the railway station and its goods yard. The rigid social distinctions of the Victorian age were still pronounced when we arrived. Neither London Road nor the houses either side of it have changed all that much since the early 1940s until now but I suspect that the distinctions are less than they were. (See the Story of Alderley Edge on the Manchester Museums website, www.Alderleyedge.Manchester. museum/theme_content, etc.)

Our arrival there on that Sunday morning in early July 1940 defined our lives for the next five years. Indeed it was to define my subsequent life and that of my parents. Whilst the children were taken off by their newly found foster parents, my parents and I were taken off in a chauffer driven car to our new home. We were billeted with one of Alderley Edge's richest families at a large villa up on the hill. We found ourselves dwellers in a no-man's land between the various social groups that divided the village and indeed the various strata within the servants of the great house. I have no doubt that the family that took in the headmaster of an evacuated school meant well but my parents found it galling to be paraded as that family's 'war effort'. We were in an invidious 'between stairs' position. We were given a small north-facing kitchen/living room and a bedroom on the same level as the family, but we were considered below them in social status. We were to use the servants' staircase that led past the kitchen and the servants' wing, but we were considered too highly placed to be welcome there. We felt very isolated, especially my mother who was at home in the one room for much of the time. We were a fair walk from the village and were isolated socially from it by reason of living up on the Edge. It took a long time for my parents to make friends. For me, I had the run of much of the great house so long as I kept away from the family. This introduced me to a world of books, of art, and music, something for which I am thankful. Isolated as I was, I could enjoy the company of the gardeners. The war had reduced the number of these to five. They were mostly older men who had learned their trade in late Victorian days and I learned from them much of traditional gardening techniques and I gained a love of plants, something that has helped shape my life. Although I was allowed to play with the head gardener's son who was close to my age, he was not allowed in the great house. On the other hand, I was not allowed to have other boys, either from Torteval or the village, to play with me in its extensive grounds.

I mention these things, not to criticise the generosity of our hosts but to give some idea of the stresses under which my parents lived and under which my father endeavoured to look after the evacuees. His approach to the situation was to keep them occupied, after all it was still term time and lessons had to go on! The day after our arrival he went to the neighbouring village of Wilmslow and met with various education officials then, on the following two days, he visited the billets of the evacuees and sorted out problems such as identity cards. There were further visits to education officials and nearby schools to beg for equipment and arrange for re-opening the school. Money was also a problem and the Log Book notes a visit to the nearby town of Macclesfield to try and sort out money arrangements. All these visits were by bus as being the only way to travel. I have never known what arrangements my father did make regarding either our personal finances or those of the other evacuees, this was surely a problem in itself as Guernsey had become isolated on 30th June and in those days banking transactions were generally done by post. Cash points or credit cards were many years away! He told me that he brought with him a collection of sterling silver spoons that he had won at air rifle shooting. At that time these were quite valuable for the metal that they contained. Whether he sold them to obtain cash or pawned them, I do not know. What is evident is that he had problems ensuring that there were enough funds available to care for the needs of the evacuees.

In the event, we resumed schooling at 'Norwood' on Monday 15th July, a week after our arrival at Alderley Edge. It was one of the villas built in the 19th century and was situated on Macclesfield Road in an area seen as somewhat socially inferior to the greater villas built on the Edge. He notes that there was little equipment, few books, and that 17 seniors were sat around a table tennis table, eleven upper juniors in a small connecting room with the remaining infants and lower juniors under the charge of Miss Grace Corbet. There was scarcely any equipment other than a few books scavenged at Rochdale or bought there at Woolworth's. The Log Book recalls a lot of activity for that first day. 21 stray Guernsey children joined us. A covering letter from Mr J. P. Robert, dated 5th July, headed 'The Controlling Committee of the States of Guernsey, Royal Court House, Guernsey c/o Ministry of Health, Manchester", placed them under the control of my father. The names of those children are given in Plate 6. 'Norwood', formerly a large home, was now an evacuation school and also accommodated Alderney States School and two schools from Manchester. Mr Jones, a H.M. Inspector of Schools called and also Mr. Armstrong, a billeting officer. I often heard the latter's name mentioned by my father. One item discussed was air raid precautions, generally referred to as ARP. We were to become familiar with air raids and the need to take cover in the cellars beneath the house whenever the warning siren sounded.

Schooling lasted from 9.00 a.m. until noon and onwards from 1.30 p.m. until 4.00 p.m., or 3.30 p.m. for the infants. Fortunately, perhaps, the Education Officer, Chester, visited the next day and he suggested that until the end of term there should be more emphasis on recreation. Accordingly various activities were organised including a cricket match that was later stopped by a thunderstorm. So work and games continued until term ended on 29th July. In those days this was the usual time of year for the summer term to end. The August Bank Holiday fell on the first Monday of August and this marked the start of the week or so of holiday enjoyed by many factory workers. The school re-opened only two weeks later. Whether this was usual in Cheshire, or because of wartime conditions, I do not know. The Log Book records that during those last weeks of the summer term, my father went to neighbouring schools to try and get further books and equipment, and that various children were claimed by their parents as noted in Plate 4.

The school re-opened on Monday 12th August and there was a visit from the school dentist. My father records elsewhere in the Log Book that the family where we were billeted paid for the treatment and indeed contributed in other ways towards the welfare of the Guernsey evacuees. The Log Book also records that the children of the village Church Sunday School gave up their Sunday School treat in order to entertain the evacuees.

An interesting entry at this point suggests that payments were being sorted out and notes salary payments as follows: F. H. Le Poidevin, £360; G.Corbet, £156; C.P.Godfay, £200; I.Pouteaux, £52; M.E.Spens, £52; and G.Odell, £51. I do not know whether this was an annual rate or salaries due. Readers will note that only the first two teachers mentioned were from Torteval, Mr. Godfray was headmaster of the Alderney States School, and the other three teachers were also from Alderney. Amongst my father's papers, but not with the Log Book, is a dossier of communications between Guernsey teachers and their Union concerning salaries.

It appears that there was continuing misunderstanding between the English authorities and the evacuated teachers concerning salary scales and allowances. My parents never discussed money matters with me, but I know that in those days, £1,000 per annum was considered a very substantial income and a labourer would not see much more than £5 per week, but then beer was one shilling, or 5 new pence a pint or less! Also, at that time, inflation was not known and most articles had their prices incorporated into their printed labels.

The Log Book continues into the autumn noting arrival of more equipment, visits by the school nurse, air raid warnings interrupting classes with children going to the cellars, more children leaving either claimed by parents or upon reaching leaving age, a child breaking a wrist by falling off a swing, more visits by education officials and so forth. There is an interesting entry for 22nd October. It relates to a visit to BBC Manchester that was preparing a programme to broadcast to the now occupied Channel Islands. I went to Manchester on the occasion, my first trip in a double-decker bus. I remember recording a message for that programme but I also recall Manchester as it then was, narrow cobbled streets filled with the noise of trams. Two months later just before Christmas, from our billet on the top of the Edge, we could see the night sky lit up by the flames of Manchester ablaze during the blitz. (Air raids at that time were usually by night). When we went there next much of what we had seen was reduced to rubble and what were shops were now open spaces. Alderley Edge, although only ten miles away was never a specific target.

My father notes that on 7th December we were invited to a puppet show at the Village School given by an Austrian refugee. He makes the comment that 'the show was a great success, and the laughter produced must have been a real tonic to the children, who at this Christmastide are thinking of their loved ones, the majority of whom are in Guernsey'. The term ended just a few days before Christmas on 20th December. The village provided a number of treats for the evacuees over that Christmas period, some at the expense of the family where my parents and I were billeted. School resumed on 6th January, by then winter had set in and the Log Book notes that the temperature inside the school was 38°F. It was, I recall, a bitterly cold winter worse than anything we from Guernsey had ever experienced. Clothing was a problem, it was in short supply and was expensive and we had left Guernsey in the height of summer carrying but one change of clothes. I have enduring memories of cold hands and feet, frozen breath, and chilblains. An entry for 22nd January noted that the school was using too much coal but also that the previous day a schools inspector had recorded the classroom temperature at 10.30 a.m. as being 44°F!

I digress here to mention problems with a particular boy whom I shall identify as S. For whatever reason he gave difficulties to one foster parent after another and at later stages was examined by medic after medic, by one social worker after another, and sent from institution to institution. My father felt it his duty to support him, he was only 7 at the time of the evacuation. Relatives were traced but were unwilling to assist because of his erratic behaviour. The Log Book has the text of a lengthy letter that my father sent to Mr Harwood, now at the Ministry of Health, Manchester. It seems that there had been discussion about sending the boy to a children's home. It is worthy of extensive quote, if only to illustrate my father's attitudes and his sense of responsibility towards the evacuees.

"Doubtless you know the boy's father and anyhow the [Guernsey family in question] is not the type to merit being sent to a 'Home'. The boy in question is at times somewhat difficult. ... He has been accused of swearing. This he has learned mainly in England, as you yourself know the Torteval and St. Pierre du Bois children 'express' themselves in "patois". Little chaps soon pick up undesirable sayings, but S is gradually learning to drop his English ways in this respect.......I would on no account permit him to be placed in a 'Home' or taken away without fighting on his behalf to my fullest powers. The boy was entrusted to me as Headmaster of Torteval School, Guernsey and evacuated by order of the States Education Council acting under Home Office orders. His both parents are in Guernsey and whatever the billeting officer may say, I look upon his welfare as under my guardianship. I told [the billeting officer] that he had no more right to suggest placing S in a 'Home' than he had the right to suggest my boy.

Some people seem to overlook the fact that however kind and generous they may be in their treatment of children, no one can replace the parental love which a young child requires....there is something lacking in an environment away from home. Last Sunday S had tea with his other little Guernsey friend at my billet and my wife can say that he was quiet and happy. The way he held my hand on the way home conveyed to me more than a child could express in words."

That last sentence typifies much of my father's attitude. He was a great believer in firm but caring parenting and had little time for professional social workers that, in his opinion, could never replace parental affection due to a child. Unfortunately problems with S continued but it is evident that my father stood by him throughout and when he was eventually put in various homes at quite some distance away from Alderley Edge, my father continued to look after his welfare to the extent of visiting him at his own expense. S returned to Guernsey after the war and I remember meeting him on a few occasions. I mention this affair of S in some detail simply to illustrate the type of problems faced by a headmaster having care of evacuated children.

Resuming my narrative in the cold early months of 1941, the Log Book notes day-to-day problems and events and contains records of many air raid warnings. There are also records of food and gifts being received from the Canadian and American Red Cross.

An entry for 8th April 1941 is of interest. Arrangements were in place for Guernsey, Alderney and Sark Children to sit special place examinations. These would be the equivalent of what is currently called the 'eleven-plus'. The subjects were mental arithmetic, written arithmetic, English and French. My father notes that the children had not seen a French textbook since leaving Guernsey in June 1940. I mention here that there was a requirement at that time for all Guernsey schools to teach the French language. I shall expand on this later. The special place examinations bore some fruit for Norman Brehaut who was awarded a scholarship to the Guernsey Boys States Intermediate School then merged with Hulme Grammar School in Oldham. My father escorted him there in October and saw him placed in his billet with a Mrs. Harrop. Both the Boys and Girls States Intermediate Schools, forerunners of the present Grammar School, as also Elizabeth College and Ladies College continued throughout the evacuation years and offered scholarship places to evacuee children. Other Torteval children, Grace Brehaut, Lois Robilliard, George Gallienne, Donald Gallienne, and the writer were later to gain scholarships.

By May 1941, contact with Guernsey was established by way of Red Cross messages and arrivals of some of these are recorded in the Log Book for that month. Loose papers within it record the heights and weights of the Torteval children, both for February 1941 and June 1942, and include copies of some of the messages that were sent by them to their parents in September 1941.

When school opened at the start of June that year, the Log Book notes that there was a return to summer clothing. That was surely welcome after the bitter winter that we had endured. It records that Barbara Savident of Le Douit, Torteval was admitted, she was daughter of John and Hilda and had been at St Peter's school. It records that Richard Stephens, who had evacuated with the school but rejoined his parents a few days later, was awarded a four-year scholarship at the Isle of Wight secondary school. An important event was the merger of some Manchester and Alderney Children with the ones from Torteval making a total of 72 children in four groups under my father, Miss Hayes, Miss Corbet, and Miss Spens, from Alderney. This merger was no doubt brought about by the resignation of Mr. Godfray, head of the Alderney School and the fact that the Manchester children had only one teacher, Miss Hayes. My father was now headmaster of the combined school. Mr R. J. Raymond, of the Alderney Society, has been in contact with me and is compiling an account of Alderney School at Alderley Edge based upon recollections of evacuees identified from this Log Book.

The record for that period speaks also of disciplinary problems such as pilfering, but not involving Torteval evacuees. It seems that these were generally resolved by my father and enclosed with the Log Book is the punishment book. Corporal punishment was quite usual in schools at that time, and when administered it was recorded. My father relied if at all possible with a good telling off. On the 7th July, the first anniversary of our arrival at Alderley Edge, my father sent letters of appreciation to various officials in the village that had given so much assistance. Summer holidays were brief, they started on 21st July and school resumed on 11th August.

One recurring problem was illness. Most children suffered at one time or another from childhood complaints such as mumps, whooping cough, and measles. This could involve stays in hospital. Another feature, common at that time, was the removal of tonsils and adenoids, a none too pleasant experience in days when ether was the usual anaesthetic. All this is detailed in the Log Book. One must remember that, at that time, medicine, as we understand it today was unknown. Antibiotics were not yet in general use nor were modern drugs. Medicines came mostly from herbal and other natural sources and dispensing chemists made up a prescription from basic materials rather than by gathering a packet from the shelf. There was not any free health service, and I hasten to put on record that the village doctors gave their services free of charge to the evacuees or had their services paid by wealthy persons in the village.

Teachers from the various Guernsey schools kept in contact with each other as far as possible. The Forest School was at Cheadle Hume, three stops away on the Manchester train. My father met with its headmaster, Mr Percy Martel from time to time. Miss Naftel, headmistress of Vauvert Girls' School visited Alderley Edge on 21st August to meet the three girls from Vauvert that were under my father's care. Mr Rawlinson, headmaster of Amherst visited later that term. During August, my father escorted two Alderney evacuees to Rochdale who had been awarded scholarships to the Girls' Intermediate School there. In those days there were a number of buses operating, but trains were used for journeys of any distance. Private cars were rare at that time and, understandably, petrol was severely rationed.

As summer was coming to an end coal was taken in for the winter heating of the school. The Log Book notes that my father and some senior boys shifted six tons of coal and seven tons of coke. Some boys also had time off to assist with digging potatoes before the winter frosts set in. These were destined for the school canteen that provided us with a cooked midday meal each day. During that September John, Eunice, and Roy Gallienne joined us. John, the eldest, had been with St Peter's Senior Boys' School whilst the younger two were from Torteval Junior. They had been with their mother in Stockport, but their billet was unsuitable. It may have been the one that I remember visiting with my father in a back-to-back terraced house opening directly onto the street. To make up for the short summer holiday there was a three-week holiday in October. The Log Book records the arrival and distribution of American and Canadian war relief clothing. One amusing entry for that period is that Walter Brehaut along with two of the older non-Torteval boys were given time off school for potato picking. The first day went well, but the second day they went off playing on nearby sand hills. They received a severe reprimand!

On 19th December, school closed for Christmas 1941 with carols and prayers. This cannot have been a happy Christmas for my parents. A few days earlier, the Japanese had bombed Pearl Harbour. This drew the USA into the war not only with Japan but also with its German ally. As children we had little understanding of the implications of all this. I am sure that my parents wondered what would be the future for all of us at Alderley Edge. Hong Kong surrendered on Christmas Day and Singapore fell a few weeks later. The German forces advanced in North Africa and they occupied Vichy France. The first part of 1942 was possibly the darkest days of the war. Victory seemed to be within the grasp of Germany and Japan. Then the tide started to turn, at first slowly, towards the end of 1942. On the bright side for us children, at Christmas 1941 we each received two shillings from the American Red Cross whilst my father gave each child sixpence in place of a Christmas card. We also were given a Christmas Party by the WVS.

What was to be our last term at Norwood started early in January with visits by H M Inspector, the school dentist, and the school nurse. There were heavy falls of snow during that month but on the brighter side, George Gallienne, Donald Gallienne, and also John Adams (ex-Amherst) were awarded scholarships to the States Intermediate School, attached to Hulme Grammar School, Oldham. My father escorted them there on 6th February. Two Jersey boys, Thurston and Vernon Collins, joined us on 9th February. As far as I recall they remained with us for much of the war. Thurston later was awarded a scholarship at Elizabeth College, then located at Great Hucklow near Buxton in Derbyshire. I remained in contact with him for a while after the war. He eventually took over his father's stationery business in St. Helier.

By mid-February it became known of a decision to close 'Norwood' and transfer the Channel Island Children to Alderley Edge Council School. As already mentioned, the war was still going badly from the Allies point of view. In January 1942 a circular was issued concerning the possible use by the enemy of poison gas when attacking Britain. It contained details of symptoms and treatment. Then on 20th March a confidential order was received from the Cheshire Education Authority concerning procedures in the event of a German invasion of Britain. Copies of these are enclosed in the Log Book and the texts are reproduced in Plates 7 and 8. Their issue shows the state of alert that existed early in 1942. At that time, or maybe earlier, signposts were removed as well as such things as name boards on railway stations to make things more difficult for invaders and the government ran various campaigns to keep things as secret as possible - 'careless talk costs lives'.

School reopened for the 1942 summer term on 13th April. The same day a letter arrived from Mr. Oldfield, leader of the Government Evacuation Scheme, to the effect that Channel Island evacuees and staff must transfer from Norwood Temporary School to Alderley Edge Council School with effect from 20th April. We were now under the control of its headmaster, Mr Twigg. The last substantial entry in the Log Book records that all the Channel Island children attended there on that day. There was no legal reason for my father to keep the Log Book after that date because, to all intents and purposes, Torteval School was no more. Nevertheless, he did include comments in it relating to further events concerning Torteval children and I shall refer to these along with some enclosures in my next section.

However, I mention now one such enclosure, a scrap of paper with the names of Guernsey, not necessarily Torteval children that were presumably admitted to Alderley Edge Council School subsequent to the merger. These are as follows:- Rumens Edward, admitted 11.5.42, left 19.6.42; Le Poidevin, Edward, admitted 18.5.42, left 18.11.42; Robilliard, Margaret and Robilliard, Neville, admitted 11.8.42; Vidamour, Margaret, admitted 1.2.43; Le Page, Marion, admitted 5.4.43, left 26.5.44; Mahé, Jean, admitted 21.12.43; and Harris, Pamela, admitted 6.4.44.

In closing this section, I record that my first days of official schooling were spent as an infant of Torteval School established at 'Norwood'. My lasting memories of those early days under Miss Corbet are those of religious education. The first things that I remember learning at school were the Lord's Prayer, in French, and the Ten Commandments, in English. We also learned about the content of the Holy Bible. 70 years on the fruits of this early learning remain very much in my mind. Christianity was the foundation of the education that we received in those days and it influenced the behaviour of the then younger generation in Torteval. This teaching of the basics of the Christian Faith in all Island schools remained part of the law of Guernsey until 1970. The repeal of this requirement by the States has been, in my opinion, to the lasting detriment of our island society.

6. *List of Guernsey children that joined Torteval School at Alderley Edge on 18 July 1940. These were children that became separated from their own schools during the course of the evacuation and were sent to Alderley Edge and placed under the care of the Headmaster of Torteval. The arrangements were made by Mr J.P. Robert, one of the three Guernsey civil servants who were sent to England by the Royal Court to care for the needs of the evacuees.*

Name	Age	School	Guernsey address
Canivet, Dorothy	9	Mont Plaisant	13 Pedvin Str. SPP.
Canivet, Katrina	13	Do.	Do.
Chippendale, Elsie	11	Vauvert	31 Pedvin Str. SPP
Ellard, Gertrude	5	Vauvert	2 Havelet SPP
Ellard, Elizabeth	6	Do.	Do.
Ellard, Myra	11	Do.	Do.
Gavey, Millicent	12	Do.	Do.
Gavey, Daphne	14	Do.	Do.
Duncombe, Ernest	12	Vauvert Boys	36 Pedvin Str. SPP
Duncombe, Ronald	10?	Do.	Do.
Greening, Violet	9	Vale	9 States Houses Delancey, SS.
Greening, Albert	12	SS Boys'	Do.
Mauger, Lily	13	St. Sampson's	Richmond Corner Cabin, SS.
Mauger, Wilfred	10	Vale Junior	Do.
Simon, Joan Daphne	13	St. Sampson's	La Herronière Lane SS
Simon, Isabelle Florence	9	Vale	Do.
Simon, Florence Isabelle	9	Do.	Do.
Simon, Patricia Beryl	13	St. Sampson's Girls	Les Sauvagées SS
Simon, Ilane	6	Do.	Do.
Simon, Daphne Joan	7	Do.	Do.
Mauger, Mildred	5	SS Infants	?

7. Transcript of printed notice issued by Chief Constable of Cheshire, January 1942 concerning precautions in the event of a gas attack.

THIS INFORMATION TO BE CIRCULATED AS WIDELY AS POSSIBLE

PROTECTION AGAINST BLISTER GAS

When attacking this Country the enemy may use poison gas. Bombs filled with liquid gas may be dropped. These will form craters which will be saturated both in and around with brown oily liquid which slowly vapourises. It is also possible that low-flying aircraft will release gas in the form of spray which will fall to the ground in tiny drops.

Two liquid gases may be used :- (1) Mustard Gas. (2) Lewisite. (1) Mustard gas smells of garlic or onions. (2) Lewisite smells of geraniums.

Either of these in liquid or vapour form will injure any part of the body with which it comes into contact, causing irritation and perhaps blisters. Successful treatment depends upon speed of application.
Dab off any visible liquid with rags. Take care not to spread about on the skin.
Used rags are dangerous - destroy them.

After dabbing liquid off, apply Anti-gas Ointment No. 1 or No. 2 or Bleach Cream. Anti-gas Ointment No. 1 and Bleach Cream will irritate the skin if left on. After using either of these the affected part must be well washed with water.

Anti-gas Ointment No. 2 will not irritate the skin so long as it is not bandaged.
Anti-gas Ointment No. 2 can be bought from Chemists NOW.
Bleach Cream and explanatory posters will be outside Chemists' shops in an emergency.
Apply ointment by rubbing until absorbed and then washing with water.
Apply bleach cream by rubbing in for one minute, leaving on for another minute and then wiping off, afterwards washing with water.

DO NOT GET EITHER OINTMENT OR CREAM IN YOUR EYES

Eyes which have been exposed to blister gas should be washed AT ONCE with warm water or a weak solution of salt or bi-carbonate of soda (a teaspoonful of either in a pint of warm water). When bathing eyes do not let the water run from the affected to the unaffected eye as it may spread the gas.

Eyes can be washed by :- (1) an eye irrigator; (2) immersing in a bowl containing warm water or one of the above-mentioned solutions; (3) a gentle stream of water from a tap, kettle or other utensil.

Do not go to a public Cleansing Station unless there is nowhere else you can possibly go. Public Cleansing Stations are primarily for persons who have been injured as well as contaminated.

If you are only contaminated you can easily treat yourself at home or in the house of a friend.

If you are unable to get home or to the house of a friend ask a Policemen or Warden for the whereabouts of the nearest Chemist's shop or Public Cleansing Station.

At the Public Cleansing Station you will receive the necessary treatment.

Outside the Chemist's shop you will find buckets of Bleach Cream. After using it go to your home or that of a friend, take off your clothes and wash all over with soap and water (preferably warm).

Contaminated clothing and footwear are dangerous and must always be left outside: NEVER taken into confined places such as shelters.

If during a raid you hear gas rattles sounding, keep under cover and put on your respirator.

The respirator protects your face and breathing passages against all known war gases.

J. BECKE
Chief Constable of Cheshire
County Controller

Civil Defence Department
CHESTER   24. 1. 42.

Printed and Published by the Cheshire Constabulary, Cheshire.

8. Transcript of Circular No: 22/1942 sent by the Director of Education, Cheshire County Council Education Department to the Head Teachers of Schools. Originally dated 30th January 1942 and subsequently redated 18th March 1942.

Dear Sir/Madam,

THE POSITION OF SCHOOLS IN THE EVENT OF INVASION

I am to inform you that, in accordance with instructions received from the Board of Education, in the event of an invasion, Day Schools in the area of operations and (as may be necessary) in areas immediately adjacent, will be closed. The actual instructions for closure will be issued to the Authority by the regional Commissioner.

In order that these instructions may be carried out promptly, the necessary information will be conveyed either by Messenger direct to the Schools or to the Clerks of the Administrative Sub-Committees and Clerks to Governors of Secondary Schools, who will immediately take steps to transmit the same to the Schools concerned. If notification is by Messenger, he or she must be requested to produce for inspection, his or her National Identity Registration Card in order to verify that the Messenger possesses the requisite authority.

A proportion of the teachers might, in the emergency, be employed upon urgent duties in connection with the Home Guard, Civil Defence, etc. It is therefore, requested that Head Teachers will at once complete the enclosed Form (in duplicate) giving the names and private addresses of those Teachers available for service with the children, one copy being forwarded to the Director of Education, County Education Office, City Road, Chester, and one copy being forwarded to the Clerk of the Administrative Sub-Committee or Clerk to the Governors of the Secondary Schools concerned.

It is very important that care should be taken by Heads of Schools to notify immediately any changes of names and private addresses so that the lists may be kept up to date.

The functions of Teachers in the emergency will depend upon whether the Schools remain open or are closed. In the former event, those teachers who remain available for service with the children will carry on the normal work of schools to the best of their ability. In the event of closure there will be many tasks to which teachers can usefully put their hands, such as visits to the children's homes, organising some sort of home tuition, using their influence to combat rumours and to allay any signs of panic, and generally by their example to maintain the morale of the neighbourhood.

It is important that conditions should remain normal as long as possible, and schools should not be closed except in very grave local emergency unless an order to close is received from, or on behalf of, the Regional Commissioner. It should be impressed upon parents by Head Teachers, that they should send their children regularly to school as long as the school is open and they should be assured that the school would not be kept open if attendance would expose their children needlessly to danger. Distribution of milk should be maintained wherever possible.

The Administrative Sub-Committees and Governing Bodies of Schools should consider what action might be taken in the event of conveyance by road and/or railway becoming impossible. Arrangements might have to be made for pupils who go to school at a distance to continue their education at some place within walking distance of their homes.

The conditions which may obtain in the event of invasion cannot be accurately forecast, but the Board have expressed the opinion that they do not doubt that they can rely on all concerned to comply readily with any instructions that may emanate from competent authorities and use their own initiative in dealing with unforeseen contingencies.

The foregoing paragraphs relate primarily to day schools, different considerations arise in the case of residential schools. The Government's view is that such schools, in common with other classes of the population, should conform to the policy of "Stay put and carry on", i.e. they should keep their pupils unless they receive instructions to the contrary from competent authorities.

Yours faithfully,

F.F.POTTER
Director of Education.

Part Three

EXPECTATION

Integration with the village school was not too difficult because the majority of evacuees were billeted in the parts of the village where the children also went to the council school. The social structure of the village was such that children from the west of the main road, the terraced houses built for the servant classes, attended the council school. Those to the east, in the area occupied by the lower middle class professionals, as likely as not went to a private school. Children of the social elite on the hill would have attended grammar schools in Manchester or Macclesfield or been sent to a public school.

By that stage, my father had become integrated into village life. At the early days of the evacuation he became an Air Raid Warden. This involved him going out night after night with his blackout torch and helmet whenever an air raid warning siren sounded. His duties included seeing that everything was properly blacked out lest a scrap of light be visible to enemy aircraft. He was required to assist if a property were bombed, something that fortunately did not occur in the village. I recall many nights spent in the cellars beneath our billet, the family duly apart from its servants. Others will remember nights spent huddled in air raid shelters. His duties as an air raid warden brought my father in contact with many from the village. Such contacts increased as he took an active part in developing allotments by using his many years of experience in growing food for the family. Allotments were part of the Government's 'Dig for Victory' campaign that encouraged as many as possible to grow their own food. In fact, when we left Alderley Edge in 1945, he was presented with a tankard, which I retain, in appreciation of his services to its Allotment Association. His contacts with villagers both as an Air Raid Warden and through the allotments meant that he was no stranger to the villagers when he joined the teaching staff at the Council School. I think that most of the evacuees integrated well because of their established contacts with the village. On the debit side, the integration with the village school, coinciding as it did with the poor progress of the war and the thoughts of a possible invasion suggested that we might remain in Alderley Edge for many years to come. As an aside, I note that amongst my father's papers was a copy of the local paper of 7th July 1944 that reported the village school sports day and listed Joyce Queripel and David Gallienne amongst the prizewinners.

Miss Spens left the teaching staff at the time of the integration, and Miss Corbet left in the October to take up a post at Old Colwyn in North Wales. My father became one of the teaching staff at the village school and taught one of its senior classes. One thing that he insisted upon was that the evacuees be taught French. Until a change of the law in 1970, when the States decided to adopt a similar education system to that in England, there was a requirement to teach French in all Guernsey schools. My father, who like many Guernsey teachers of his generation had attended a course at Caen University on teaching French as a foreign language, continued to teach French to the evacuees. Unfortunately, perhaps, he was not a Patois speaker so, unlike Mr. Walter Brehaut who evacuated with the St. Pierre du Bois children, he was unable to keep alive what was for many children of those days their first language. His lack of knowledge of Patois was a disappointment to the Torteval Douzaine who had hoped that his replacement of the former headmaster,

Captain Boon, would ensure a Patois speaker. The reasons for his lack of knowledge were twofold. His own father, himself a native speaker of Patois, married a non-Patois speaker and so English was the language used in the home. The second reason, common to many of his generation, was a feeling that the use of Patois was not the mark of good education and therefore should be avoided. As an aside, he did learn a few Patois expressions, but not what he thought they meant, presumably from older Torteval boys. These produced considerable embarrassment when he used them in front of my wife's family. Nobody dared tell him what they meant nor would I wish to explain further!

My first few months were spent in the Infant School under a Miss Benison but principally under Miss Turner. I was put in contact with Miss Turner, who remained a spinster, about ten years ago by some friends of hers who visited Guernsey. She lived to a ripe old age and we corresponded. She was a highly intelligent lady and became a Justice of the Peace. From the infant school I moved on to first year juniors under Mr 'Pop' Ellis, a Cornishman. My memories of him relate to his frequent and brutal use of the cane, a common teaching aid in those days. From there I moved to my father's class prior to being awarded a scholarship to Elizabeth College. I moved to its junior school at Great Hucklow in Derbyshire in September 1944. This had the effect of isolating me both from the evacuees and also the village boys at Alderley Edge.

Slowly, and at first almost as imperceptibly as the tide at Portelet begins its rise after low water, the tide of war changed. In October 1942, the advance of the German forces towards the Suez Canal was halted at El Alamein and in the following month Tobruk was recaptured. Into 1943, the remaining Axis forces in North Africa surrendered and German submarines ended their harassment of North Atlantic convoys. Later that year German forces in Russia were in retreat and allied forces landed in Sicily. In September Italy surrendered to the allies with a subsequent change of sides. In the Far East too there were signs that Japan was contained. In the meantime, American forces had arrived in Britain and we saw many of these at Alderley Edge and learned to ask 'Any gum, chum?' Also, for most of us evacuees we saw Negroes for the first time as some were serving in the US forces. This might seem a surprising remark to modern readers, but in those days persons of a different race were a rarity in Guernsey and generally in Britain. That might account for the fact that in Guernsey of some 70 years ago, racism was unknown to us. In fact, to this day I cannot understand racist attitudes because racism was not part of my upbringing.

As fortunes of the allies continued to grow and increase in pace, as does the tide as it approaches half-tide, so we began to think of allied victory as an outcome and the gloom of 1942 receded. My parents now had the confidence to travel and we visited my maternal cousin in North Wales and I saw and played in the sea for the first time in three or more years. We saw signs of more and more troop activity and in early summer 1944 we noticed convoys of army lorries moving south through Alderley Edge and one day we found that the Americans had left. The news of the Normandy landings reached us in early June 1944 and raised our expectations and morale. As news came through of the success of those landings, and later of the recapture of Cherbourg, the Cotentin, and Saint Malo we felt that the liberation of Guernsey was imminent. Those remaining in Guernsey shared the same hopes. A most interesting enclosure with the Log Book is a draft letter by my father to Reverend Greenhow dated initially 17th June 1944. It was written in the expectation of an imminent return to Guernsey. I reproduce it in full in Plate 9. What is so poignant about it is the fact that the draft was amended and redated 4th May 1945. This demonstrates more than anything else the hopes of June 1944 and our subsequent wait of nearly a year until liberation.

Just as the speed with which the tide rises falls off as high water is approached, so also both those of us evacuees and those remaining in Guernsey faced a long and agonising wait. I think that we all expected either a surrender of the German occupying forces or the landing of a liberating task force. From the German point of view, the situation is covered admirably in the Occupation Diary of Baron von Aufsess[2] a non-Nazi who had the responsibility of liaison between the German military and the local authorities. Cruickshank[1], in his account, mentions the attitude taken by Churchill and his famous or infamous 'Let 'em rot!' minute by which he dismissed any thought of liberating the Islands. For many years this was kept hidden and we did not realise the hollow words of his VE day speech when he said that 'Our dear Channel Islands are to be freed to-morrow'. When others and I heard it at school on 8th May 1945 we did not realise the suffering endured by those in Guernsey who had faced an additional year of occupation and deprivation.

The expectations and frustrations of my parents are also illustrated by a series of newspaper clippings retained within the Log Book. An article in *The Times* of 5th December 1944 is headed 'Channel Islands "Nightmare" – Resident's story of sufferings – earnest plea for aid'. It reproduces a letter from a Jersey lady dated 2nd October that year. How it reached her mother in London is not known, although after the liberation of the Cotentin, it was but a few miles from Jersey to there. It describes the situation in Jersey, their sufferings, fears, and anxieties, their fears for the winter, their meagre rations and the black market in food. It continues 'Tell them at home to come and relieve us. We would willingly put up with the bombing and would help all we can if only we could be free....We all feel that we have been abandoned by the

Mother Country….There has never been one message over the BBC or anything in over four and a half years….If we had been French, Polish, or any other nationality, we would have been showered with messages and pamphlets. But because we are British we are thoroughly neglected and nobody at home seems to care a hoot….His Majesty sent a delightful message dated June 14, 1940 [i.e. before the German invasion] and do you know that it was given no publicity by the States and thousands of people never heard it….The message would have given great comfort to thousands…It appears that it was deliberately suppressed….The disappointment of not being rescued is terrible…We were all keyed up and looking forward to being released after Avranches and St Malo fell. We were overjoyed as the sound of guns drew nearer and nearer….then nothing happened and the sound of guns went further and further away….I hear that a question was asked about us in the House of Commons this week, and that the reply was "The garrisons of Jersey and Guernsey were given a chance to surrender, but refused. There was no reason to suppose that the inhabitants are not being properly treated" and that was all'. Without wishing to comment upon the truth of the contents of that letter quoted in *The Times*, imagine the effect upon my parents and any other evacuees who might have read it. I wonder how they passed on such news, if at all, to the evacuee children or answered their questions should they have heard it from others?

It was not only *The Times* that contained such articles. Some more popular newspapers carried articles in a similar vein. On 23rd November 1940 the *Daily Sketch* disclosed that 70,000 people in the German-occupied Channel islands are faced with starvation and makes an impassioned plea to send food to the Islands. In a somewhat more flamboyant article, on 27th November the *Daily Mail* portrayed the plight of the Channel Islanders and speaks of the hope of relief by way of ships in

Lisbon, (Portugal remained neutral during WW2). The article says that 'These Britons want food, clothing, food and medical supplies, but most of all they need the moral support of the British Government. They long for a gesture of sympathy from the British people, even were it only the dropping of a few newspapers over the islands or the broadcasting of a few messages over the wireless…'. The article continues in lurid detail describing children in rags, no anaesthetics, bramble tea, and Germans eating horses. With the benefit of hindsight historians may say that this account was exaggerated, however the issue is the effect that it would have had on the many evacuees who read this popular newspaper. On a more sober note in an editorial in the *Manchester Guardian* of the same date, attention was drawn to how in the days immediately after the Normandy landings Channel Island evacuees in Britain were rejoicing and expected that the Germans would consider their possession to be untenable and would quietly depart. It continued by remarking that 'the Germans there are our prisoners; but they are still the gaolers of our people'. The editorial ended on a more optimistic note that 'two ships are lying in Lisbon Harbour loaded with Red Cross food parcels and clothes and medicinal supplies …. Whether they are allowed to land their cargoes without hindrance ….depends on a German decision'.

Such was the information that greeted evacuees shortly before Christmas 1944. Although the end of the war, at least in Europe, appeared much closer, there was obvious worry and anxiety amongst the evacuees who had hoped since the previous June for a speedy return home. This worry clearly continued until shortly before the Liberation. A cutting from the *Daily Mail* dated 1st March 1945 spoke of conditions in Jersey as described by five men who had recently escaped from there. It describes a desperate shortage of fuel and the use of wind power and primitive generators to obtain electricity. It comments upon the serious shortage of food with the Germans, in similar difficulties, capturing cats and dogs for meat. It notes that some islanders collaborate with the occupying force. On a more positive note it describes the arrival of a Red Cross ship with food parcels. (For an account of the Channel Islands in the closing days of the occupation, I refer you again to Cruickshank[1] and von Aufsess[2]). Without commenting upon the truth or otherwise of such an article in a widely read daily newspaper, I do comment that it could only have had an unsettling effect upon all evacuees that read it.

One of the miscellaneous entries made after the merger with the Council School is a very sad one. On 18th September 1942, my father notes that he returned from his first holiday since leaving Guernsey to find that Roy Gallienne was seriously ill and was removed to Stockport Infirmary for observation. He had been caught in the rain and developed chest trouble. He died at the end of October with his mother beside him. My father attended the funeral on 5th November along with Roy's brother John and his sister Eunice. I recall Roy's death, he was about my age and a friend at school. It was my first experience of the death of somebody that I knew. In this day and age one might ask why should a child of 8 years or so die after getting soaked in the rain? One reason would be that we were all somewhat undernourished, but more pertinently antibiotics, although known, were in the early stages of development and were not available.

Other post April 1942 entries generally concern children leaving and these are included in the Table found in Plate 4.

One comment that I would make is about the generally carefree childhood that we spent at Alderley Edge, carefree that is apart from the separation from Guernsey. At that time there were very few private cars or other vehicles and people simply did not travel around and about for pleasure.

Consequently, the roads were very safe and there was not any question of people travelling around looking for trouble or preying upon youngsters. With the absence of television or Internet and with very few magazines and a restrained Press there was no noticeable dissemination of bad or promiscuous ideas. We travelled freely and fearlessly when quite young. For example at the age of ten, I was able to travel on my own by train from Alderley Edge to Miller's Dale, the nearest station to Great Hucklow. This included changes of trains at Stockport and Buxton. Youngsters travelling alone over longer distances generally did so under the care of the guard. Also, at the age of ten, I sometimes spent my pocket money on a bus ride to Manchester with friends simply to have a look around. Neither my parents nor I had any cause for concern and if there were problems one could always ask a policeman or staff at a railway station. Similarly, when boarding with Elizabeth College at Great Hucklow, as ten or eleven year -olds, we were allowed to go for Tuesday afternoon walks of several miles across the moors or to other villages. Security was never considered a problem. We learned to be self-reliant and we were brought up free from the modern Nanny State.

9. Transcript of a draft letter handwritten by Headmaster to Reverend Greenhow, Rector of Torteval, originally dated 17th June 1944 and amended on 4th May 1945.

Alderley Edge Council School,
Alderley Edge,
Nr. Manchester,

June 17th 1944

(May 4/45)

Dear Rev. Greenhow,

The Headmaster and Children of Torteval School are glad to have their opportunity to pay their sincere respects to the Bailiff of Guernsey, States Education Council, You and Mrs. Greenhow and Committee, Teachers, children, parents of Torteval.

All looking forward most eagerly to speedy reunion and sight of our beloved Island home.

Norman, Grace Brehaut - Donald, George Gallienne, Loïs Robilliard Jean Vidamour all well at Intermediate.

David Gallienne, Oswald Torode, Walter Robilliard, Madelaine Brehaut, Joyce Queripel, André Paint very fit. Walter Brehaut, Nicholas Robilliard splendid young men — making efficient farmers. John Gallienne assistant groundsman Cricket Club, okay. Eunice with mother now.

Barbara Savident fine, working similar Creasey's. Kenneth Le Prevost, gardener, excellent lad, Renée

Gouasdoué, maid, nice situation. Elsie
Chippendale orthopaedic hospital, Gobowen,
Oswestry. Hip joint trouble. Specialist
treatment. Hopeful permanent cure. Writing first
opportunity.

Mrs. Elsie Robilliard, Neville, Mrs. Miriam
Robilliard, Margaret, Mrs. Elsie Vidamour,
Margaret, Mrs. Erena Chalmers, Anne, Mrs Adèle
Le Page, Marion same village. All well. Love.

Miss Grace Corbet very fit. Cripple School, Old
Colwyn. Greetings.

Four years is a long time in a child's life.
They have endeared themselves to their foster
parents in Alderley Edge, for whom I have
nothing but praise for the way in which they
have cared for our children. Their kindness (I
include the Billeting Officers and the local
Headmasters) can never be repaid. They all send
their best wishes to parents, whom they feel
they know.

I have often dreamt of our reunion and trust
that it will be a happy reality in the near
future.

Mrs. Le Poidevin, Nicholas *now at Elizabeth
College* and I send our love to our parents and
families.

Yours sincerely,
Frank H Le Poidevin

Rev. E. N. Greenhow,
The Rectory,
Torteval
Guernsey C.I.

Part Four

EPILOGUE

In September 1944 I started in Form II at Elizabeth College. Since 1940, its Infant and Junior Schools were housed in various buildings at Great Hucklow, a small isolated village in the Peak District between Buxton and Sheffield. What is relevant to this narrative is that schooling away from Alderley Edge isolated me not only from the friends that I had made in that village but also from the Guernsey children living there. That is a feature of moving schools or localities, friends that one made are often lost and the intimacy that one once had is seldom recovered.

We received news of the German surrender on May 8th 1945 and were given a day off. I spent it with the late Peter Blackmore walking across the moors in the rain to Grindleford some 5 miles away. That evening we listened to Winston Churchill's broadcast and rejoiced to hear that 'our dear Channel Islands will be freed to-morrow'. Within days I was receiving from and sending letters to my grandparents, aunts, and uncles. Sadly, the first letter that I received from Guernsey told of my paternal grandfather's death nine days after the Liberation. Within weeks boys were being told that arrangements were being made for their return to Guernsey and one by one they left as others waited their turn. One afternoon I was told to pack and the following morning taken to Miller's Dale and put on a train to Manchester where my parents met me and took me to Alderley Edge where I spent some days awaiting our return.

Because I was not with my parents when news came of the Liberation, I have no first-hand knowledge of how my father handled the effects of the long awaited news. I know that he, along with others, made a broadcast to people in Guernsey, in his case specifically to Torteval, shortly after the event. A piece of paper enclosed with the Log Book, but not in his handwriting, has, what I have only recently discovered, the text of the message that he sent:

'F. H. Le Poidevin, Headmaster
Torteval Schools, Guernsey

Greetings to Guernsey and particularly to the
Education Council, Rev & Mrs Greenhow and
Committee, Scholars and Parents.
    All children both big and small send you their
fondest love and kisses. They have been very fit,
happy and wonderfully cared for by their foster
parents during their stay at Alderley Edge.
    Children are eager for re-union with their loved
ones. All have grown in stature, wisdom and self-
reliance. Would be delighted to have photographs of
parents as first steps to re-union, which I hope will be
very soon.

From self, wife, Nicky, to our own folk. Fondest
                                                Love.
                                       Le Poidevin.'

I know that my parents attended a thanksgiving service in London. What I do not know, but can only surmise, is how my father prepared the Torteval children for their return. They had been away from their own parents for five years, in contact only by sporadic Red Cross messages. Some had left as children and were now moving into young adulthood. Others were in Infant School when they left and were now approaching the age to enter secondary school. All had spent critical formative years in Cheshire and had bonded with their foster parents. Returning to Guernsey might appear to us now as a fulfilment of five years of yearning, but it was also a time of separation from one environment and family home to return to what was something in their past. Not as brutal as the evacuation, certainly, but not without trauma. One can judge from the letter that my father had drafted to send to Reverend Greenhow, that he was very conscious of the careful guidance that would be needed. Five years is a long time in a child's life.

We left for Guernsey on Monday 23rd July, with the remnants of Torteval School. Our departure was noted in the *Alderley and Wilmslow Advertiser* of 20th July in an article that spoke of the way in which the evacuee children had endeared themselves to their foster-parents and also spoke in glowing terms of my parents' contribution to community life. I don't know what good-byes were said but my mother in particular was immensely relieved to escape the life that she had endured. It was a London train and I think that we had reserved compartments. We travelled south towards warmth and bluer skies. At Euston we were met and transported to Waterloo. I had my first sight of London with its traffic, trolley busses, and its trams emerging from the Kingsway tunnel. We had a few hours to wait at Waterloo and were given refreshments. Then the station announcer's voice told us that the Channel Islands Boat Express was standing on such and such platform. This was an emotional moment. We travelled south on a glorious summer evening and, passing through Southampton Terminus, the train crossed the road and stopped alongside the *Hantonia* that was to take us home. How different was that journey from the one five years earlier! The crossing was calm and we could sleep in berths. Because the Little Russel was not yet clear from mines, the ship went south about and in the early morning sunlight we saw the cliffs of Torteval and the spire of its Church.

When we entered the Harbour we found it almost deserted, security was even stricter then than now and the public were not allowed beyond the Weighbridge, although that was soon to change. An army sergeant led us from the New Jetty to a bus awaiting us at the Weighbridge. It was a beautiful sunny morning and we looked at the Town in excitement. The bus took us up the Ruettes Brayes and diverted along the pink coloured roads of the Ville au Roi Estate to deposit my mother and me for a tearful reunion with her parents living then at 'Braeside' in the Ville au Roi. We returned to our own home later that day, thankfully little touched because my mother's brother and family had occupied it and prevented its requisition by the German forces. Father continued out to Torteval with the bus and to the reunions there. I went with him to Torteval a day or two later. Now too large to go on the back of his bike, I think that we got there by bus and returned by hitching a lift on a tomato lorry. My memory is of my father being made so welcome by the families of the evacuees, a welcome that he and my mother experienced for the rest of their lives.

My abiding memory of summer 1945 was of days of warmth and rich blue skies. I stayed some times with my paternal aunt Hilda, who, during the war had married John Langlois of La Maison de Haut, a wonderful old Guernsey house situated in the lane behind Sion Chapel in St Peter's. The air in their greenhouses was heavy with the scent of ripening melons and grapes. Soon the cool summers of Cheshire and Derbyshire were forgotten. Guernsey started to rebuild itself but the gulf of five years could never recreate the pre-war society. Changes, innocuous enough at the time, to our system of government and to our laws of inheritance made for a new society with changing attitudes. These have led to a breakdown of family and parish life and the acceptance of very different moral standards from those prevailing in 1945 making for an entirely different Guernsey from the one to which we returned with so much anticipation.

My parents and I were the only members of our immediate family that had left the Island. Upon our return, our reception by the rest of the family was not altogether warm. For many years at family gatherings we were reminded that we ran away from the Germans whilst the rest of the family stayed and suffered. In vain would my father remonstrate that he left out of a sense of duty to the children of his school and to their parents, indeed he felt that he left with his school because that was what was required of him by the States. Some of our family could not grasp this and for years there was animosity and the closeness that existed before the war had gone. I do not believe that such situations were confined to my family and many other Guernsey families had rifts in the immediate post-war years between those that stayed and those that left.

Another source of friction was with the States. Families that remained in Guernsey were generally entitled to some form of post-war rehabilitation grant. The object was to help them regain their feet after the years of war. This was denied to my father on the basis that he had not remained in Guernsey during the war years. There may have been some logic to that approach, but my father always took the view that he went away at the request of the States Education Committee to accompany evacuated children and that he was entitled to a similar grant. I mention this not to argue the rights and wrongs of the matter but to put on record the attitude of an involuntary evacuee who felt that his devotion to duty was not recognised.

My father remained headmaster of Torteval for a short while after our return. At that stage there a decision was made to run down the School and merge it with the Forest. My father was appointed headmaster of Amherst, a post that he held until his retirement in 1964. Torteval Infants School remained open for some years but it moved to the building formerly occupied by the Junior School that has now become the Douzaine Room. Its headmistress was Miss Gladys Martel, sister of Mr Percy Martel, headmaster of the Forest. She lived in Belmont Road, St Peter Port, and travelled to Torteval each day by car. Her driving was notoriously erratic and any prudent road user would keep a safe distance!

My mother, a qualified teacher, reverted to teaching more out of necessity than desire. Keeping a teenager at Elizabeth College cost money, even when he was there as a special place holder. So my mother went back to work to help support me. Worse still, I had been fortunate to win an Open Scholarship from Elizabeth College to Oxford. It was worth more by way of prestige than money. I applied for a grant from the Education Council of the day but this was refused on the basis that anybody educated at Oxford would not be likely to return to Guernsey. Accordingly, my mother continued back at work and taught first at St Saviour's Infants and then moved to Torteval Infants, initially under Miss Martel but finally on her own. She was the last teacher at Torteval School and closed its doors finally on 25th July 1961. A photograph, reproduced with this narrative, taken on the 19th July shows its last pupils and another shows the building from which the evacuees left on 21st June 1940.

The evacuation years brought my parents very close to

Torteval and after our return to Guernsey they determined to live there. Eventually an opportunity arose to build a bungalow at Les Tielles and we moved there in 1950. Father travelled to Amherst each day by bicycle, bus, or on a 50cc motor scooter. I cycled into Town most days. Schooling at Elizabeth College was a six-day a week affair and on several days each week it did not end until 5.45 p.m., too late for the last bus! Cycling home at that time on a dark wet and windy winter night was something that one accepted. However, there were few cars and cycling in those conditions was much safer than it would be today. My parents moved into Town some years later but then returned to Torteval and lived at Le Coin near to Torteval Stores. Ultimately, they joined me just across the border in St. Peter's but, like me, they never formed any real connection with that parish preferring Torteval. In their later years they attended the Methodist Chapel and both their funerals took place there.

For my part, I owe my career to the initial schooling that I received at Torteval. This enabled me to gain scholarships first to Elizabeth College and then on to Oxford and gave to me an education that my parents could not have afforded to provide. If I am asked where I was educated, my invariable reply is at Torteval School and then onwards from there by scholarship. I am appalled that some present day deputies seek to do away with the eleven plus and special places at the Colleges. I am equally appalled that some seek to close our smaller schools. The cost of educating children in smaller schools in a caring parish environment may be higher than sending them to large schools. But the ultimate cost to the Island of not educating children in small schools or at the Colleges may well be greater.

In 1967, I married into a Torteval family. Unfortunately, my marriage to Marguerite Tostevin was comparatively short because she died in 1980 at the early age of 43. I continue to live where we enjoyed our married life but, like my parents, I have never formed any attachment to St Peter's and consider my roots to be in Torteval. Certainly one of my proudest moments was to be elected its deputy in 1985. I can only regret that modern reforms have meant that the parish no longer has either its own deputy or a Douzaine representative in the States.

I know that some evacuees from Torteval maintained contact with their foster parents and returned to Alderley Edge from time to time. For reasons that should be apparent from what I have related, my parents had no wish to return although my father wrote to our hosts on a number of occasions. My wife, Marguerite, and I visited them briefly in about 1968 when driving home from a visit to Scotland. There was some confusion as to dates and we arrived a day early. We were too late for afternoon tea and after some difficulty a young and inexperienced parlour maid was found to provide a drinks tray. Unfortunately she laid out some chocolate biscuits with the sherry and more unfortunately Marguerite took one. This led to a conversation amongst our hosts to the effect that 'if she wants to have a chocolate biscuit with her sherry we'll let her, she just doesn't know any better'. Marguerite felt humiliated and we both understood how my parents had felt. Marguerite was able to turn the tables a few minutes later. We were shown their small lean-to greenhouses. I remembered them well from the war years. The family had managed to find the coal to heat them even then. They boasted a few peaches and a few bunches of grapes struggling to ripen in the weak northern sun. Marguerite pointed out that in our home we had some much larger greenhouses full of peaches and nectarines and that her family grew about an acre of table grapes. Our visit ended fairly abruptly on that note! I cannot blame our hosts. They were generous to me and to my parents and in an anonymous way to the Torteval evacuees. Their social attitudes were, like I suppose those of all of us, fashioned by their upbringing.

My second visit was in the year 2000. I was on my own and walked around the village, retracing the steps that I took to and from school. The memories implanted in my mind were those of Alderley Edge 55 years earlier. If a person lives with changes it is difficult to recall things as they were, but here photographed in my mind were images of Alderley Edge in 1945. In many ways little had changed. The railway station, apart from electrification was much as we left it. I do not think that it had been painted since! What was noticeable was the lack of staff. In the war years it was bustling with porters, ticket collectors and others. Now it was deserted. The road past the Victorian village church, dedicated like Torteval's to St Phillip, led alongside the same privet hedge to the school, its façade unchanged. The road bridge over the railway line by the station was still there but the row of tall elm trees with their rookery had gone.

I walked past the children's playground beside the railway where we went most days after school, it was still there with its slides, swings and roundabouts. The railway was now securely fenced. In those days we sat on the fence and sometimes managed to visit the footplate of a goods engine waiting on the siding. On one memorable day a kindly driver took us aboard whilst shunting in the goods yard on the other side of the main line. (Imaging what present day Health and Safety and Child Protection Agency people would say!). The siding remains but the goods yard has gone, replaced by a supermarket.

I continued my walk past the allotments, still in use, where my father once grew vegetables. I crossed the next railway bridge and passed the brick terraced houses where some of my village friends once lived and whose mothers made me so welcome. My steps took me along my former road to home, past the Methodist chapel and the cricket field and up the hill towards the great house. Some of what were its vegetable gardens and orchards were now covered with modern housing. The house itself was scarcely visible behind the trees and, more strikingly, security fences. I saw some squirrels, not the native red ones of 50 or 60 years earlier but naturalised grey ones. My impression of the whole area of the great houses was one of high security. They are now the preserve of film stars and footballers and their wealth an attraction to predators.

I returned down the hill to the village. The general appearance of the main street had changed little. It retained its wide footpaths and sweeping curve, but it was full of traffic as it was on the A34, the main Manchester to Southampton road. Some shops were easily recognisable, there was still a chemist on one corner and a hair stylist at what was a gents' barber. The lower middle class houses were there to the east of the main road. The cottage hospital where so many of us spent some time during the evacuation days had gone. Such charitable foundations disappeared with the coming of the National Health Service. Thus was my trip down memory lane. My thoughts as I revisited those scenes were that what has passed has gone, we must live in the present. Certainly, the experience of Alderley Edge has influenced the course of my life and gone to forming its future, but one must not seek to recapture what has past, only learn from it. If one wants to stay young, one must not live in the past but in the present.

Whatever I may have thought about the effect of the occupation and the evacuation on me or my parents faded into insignificance when in 2007, coincidentally on May 9th, Liberation Day, I stood in silence with others in the gas chamber of Auschwitz. When I considered the countless thousands of men, women, and children, who were transported to that very room there to die in the agonies of cyanide poisoning, then I realised that whatever may have been the personal sufferings of Guernsey people, occupied, evacuated, or deported, these were slight compared with what so many human beings suffered simply for being Jewish, gypsy, Slavonic, mentally or physically defective, or homosexual. The lesson of World War II that we should relearn every Liberation Day is that Nazism shows us where a human society can go when it abandons the Laws of God and puts human reasoning first.

The number of us who have personal recollections of the evacuation or occupation grows smaller with every passing year. I thought it right to give my personal memories. I can now do this more freely since there are few alive who remember the evacuation and the years in Alderley Edge and I can say things that were better left unsaid in earlier years. Reports of an eyewitness are more reliable than those who rely on hearsay and I hope that this contributes something to an understanding of what took place and the effects that it had. If my opinions appear unacceptable to some, that is because they arose from the formation that I received in those five years as an evacuee.

Regrettably, persons who were not in Guernsey or evacuated have seen fit to criticise the behaviour of some Islanders during those years. I resent this deeply. War is terrible; isolation is terrible, as is the separation of children and parents for five years of uncertainty. If there were or are old scores to settle, leave it for us Islanders to sort out, we do not need to be told by outsiders how we ought to have behaved. We went through it either as occupied people, as deportees, or as evacuees; they did not. They have no right whatsoever to censure us for how we passed those five years. I give one example. There was sabotage early in 1941 when a German telephone cable near the airport was cut in two places. Jurat John Leale, in condemning this, reminded the States and the population that those who remained did so voluntarily. In an article that appeared in *The Star* on 22nd March that year he commented that on the Saturday of evacuation week in June 1940 two large vessels left the island, one practically empty and the other completely so. He went on to say that those who remained knew that the German forces might occupy Guernsey without any resistance, therefore they accepted that position and must conduct themselves as good citizens. Critics would do well to dwell on words such as these.

Those who have not passed through periods of adversity cannot appreciate how people may behave when in times of stress. It is unacceptable for people to point fingers at the way in which either islanders or evacuees behaved in those years. The behaviour of persons in Britain was not always exemplary. There was a black market operating in Alderley Edge, and many items in short supply went 'under the counter'. Astute shopkeepers in the village knew where their bread lay buttered and made sure that the wealthy up the Hill did not go short of things even if it were at the expense of the villagers as a whole. My mother had many stories of how well she was treated in a shop until the shopkeeper realised that she was buying on her own account and not for the wealthy family where we were billeted.

In concluding my narrative I cannot overemphasise the genuine care, kindness, and concern was shown to the evacuees by the ordinary working people of Rochdale during our two weeks stay there and by those of Alderley Edge for the two weeks and five years that we passed there. For this our profound gratitude and thanks remain due. On the debit side my parents were traumatised by the patronising class system that we encountered in Alderley Edge. I seldom saw my mother smile or laugh throughout the remainder of her life. In matters of class, my father's attitudes rub off on me. Guernsey society, whilst respecting people for their position in Island society, respects far more hard work and ability. Guernsey people are entitled to respect not because of who they are but because of what they are. In the Guernsey of my childhood, the more senior people in society would not look down upon the less fortunate. The English class system that now infiltrates our Island has no place here any more than has racial or religious intolerance. Guernsey people expect respect as individuals and resent being reduced to non-entities in a bureaucratic system.

I suggest that one of the main reasons that kept Torteval together during the occupation and evacuation years was because it was a small closely-knit and cohesive community centred on its Church and Chapel and on its school. The growing centralisation of government in the name of efficiency is not, in my opinion, the best for our Island. Parish deputies that were close to their parish had the interests of their people at heart. Regretfully, we now have career politicians who easily fall victim to the temptation of putting themselves first. The type of civil servants that saw Guernsey through the occupation has also disappeared. A handful of dedicated people guided the destinies both of those who remained in Guernsey and those that were evacuated. We now have a huge bureaucracy that is at risk of providing employment for itself rather than catering for the essential needs of Islanders.

I suggest that the biggest threats to modern Guernsey are firstly a failure by government and commerce to treat and respect people as individuals, something that our parish system ensured. Secondly, I believe that the modelling of our education system on that of England is to the detriment of our society. Both the loss of Christianity and the loss of the French language brought about by the Education Law of 1970 have severed us from our cultural roots. Guernsey survived the occupation and the evacuation because it was a close-knit community rooted to the land and the sea. I wonder whether current society has the cohesion to survive should the events of 1940-1945 reoccur? I leave the answer to those who read this narrative.

10　The final class at Torteval (Infants'), School taken by Grut's on 19th July, 1961, prior to its closure on 25th July, 1961.

Back row (l. to r.): Lorraine Le Tocq, Lawrence Harding, Peter Sarre, Elizabeth Falla, Mrs G. M. Le Poidevin (Teacher), Martin Ozard, Lionel Brehaut, Geoffrey Scales, Gillian de la Mare.
Absent: Malcolm de la Mare.

Front Row (l. to r.): Carole de la Mare, June Gallienne, Carol Le Cras, Susan Ashplant, Marigold Scales, Angela Brehaut, Susan Brehaut, Winifred Saunders.
Absent: Mary Brouard.

11   Torteval (Infants'), School taken by Grut's on 19th July, 1961.

ABOUT THE AUTHOR

Nicholas (Nick) Le Poidevin was six years-old at the time of the Evacuation. He was the only child of Frank Harry Le Poidevin and Gladys Mary (Jean) Le Poidevin (*née* Munro). He was enrolled at Torteval School, of which his father was Headmaster, at the time of the Evacuation. He remained with that School until autumn 1944 when he took up a scholarship at Elizabeth College. He was later awarded an Open Scholarship in Natural Science at Lincoln College, Oxford, where he obtained an Honours Degree in Agriculture specialising in crop science. From there he took up a Colonial Office Probationership at Wye College, University of London, and at the Imperial College of Tropical Agriculture, Trinidad. He served with the Colonial Agricultural Service in the Gambia and subsequently was a sugar cane agronomist in British Guiana. He returned to Europe in 1962 and obtained a Ph.D. in toxicology at the University of London. His father's failing health prompted his return to Guernsey where he taught science for some years at Elizabeth College prior to working in horticulture. Meanwhile he married Marguerite Tostevin of Myrtle Place, Torteval. They had two children, Louise and Matthieu, both now married and living in Guernsey. With the demise of the horticultural industry in Guernsey he resumed working abroad as a consultant in irrigated tropical crops, principally sugar, in the Sudan, Ethiopia, Egypt and Somalia. Subsequent to his wife's death in 1980 he returned to Guernsey to care for his children and started a new career in law. He qualified as a Barrister in 1986 and as an Advocate of the Royal Court the following year. Along with his studies he served as Deputy for Torteval from 1985-1988. He continued in practice as an Advocate until 2000. Apart from his great love of the sea and sailing, he is interested in Guernsey culture, and spends his retirement growing food and ornamental plants as well as reading theology and European history.